W9-CHR-822

READING POWER

Kobe Bryant
"Slam Dunk" Champion
Rob Kirkpatrick

The Rosen Publishing Group's
PowerKids Press ™
New York

For my sister, Casey.

Published in 2000 by The Rosen Publishing Group, Inc.
29 East 21st Street, New York, NY 10010

First Edition

Book design: Michael de Guzman

Photo Credits: pp. 5, 22 © Andrew D. Bernstein/NBA/Allsport; pp. 7, 15, 21 © Todd Warshaw/Allsport; p. 9 © David Taylor/Allsport; p. 11 © Vincent Laforet/Allsport; p. 13 © Tom Hauck/Allsport; p. 17 © Brian Bahr/Allsport; p. 19 © Aubrey Washington/Allsport.

Text Consultant: Linda J. Kirkpatrick, Reading Specialist/Reading Recovery Teacher

Kirkpatrick, Rob.
        Kobe Bryant : "slam dunk" champion / by Rob Kirkpatrick.
        p. cm. — (Reading power)
    Includes index.
    SUMMARY: Introduces Kobe Bryant, a young player for the Los Angeles Lakers basketball team.
        ISBN 0-8239-5539-7 (lib. bdg.)
        1. Bryant, Kobe, 1978– Juvenile literature. 2. Basketball players—United States Biography Juvenile literature. [1. Bryant, Kobe, 1978– 2. Basketball players. 3. Afro-Americans—Biography.] I. Title. II. Series.
        GV884.B794 K57 1999
        796.323'092—dc21
        [B]   99-32383
                                                               CIP

Manufactured in the United States of America

Contents

Kobe Bryant plays basketball. He is in the NBA.

5

Kobe is on the Los Angeles Lakers. He is number 8.

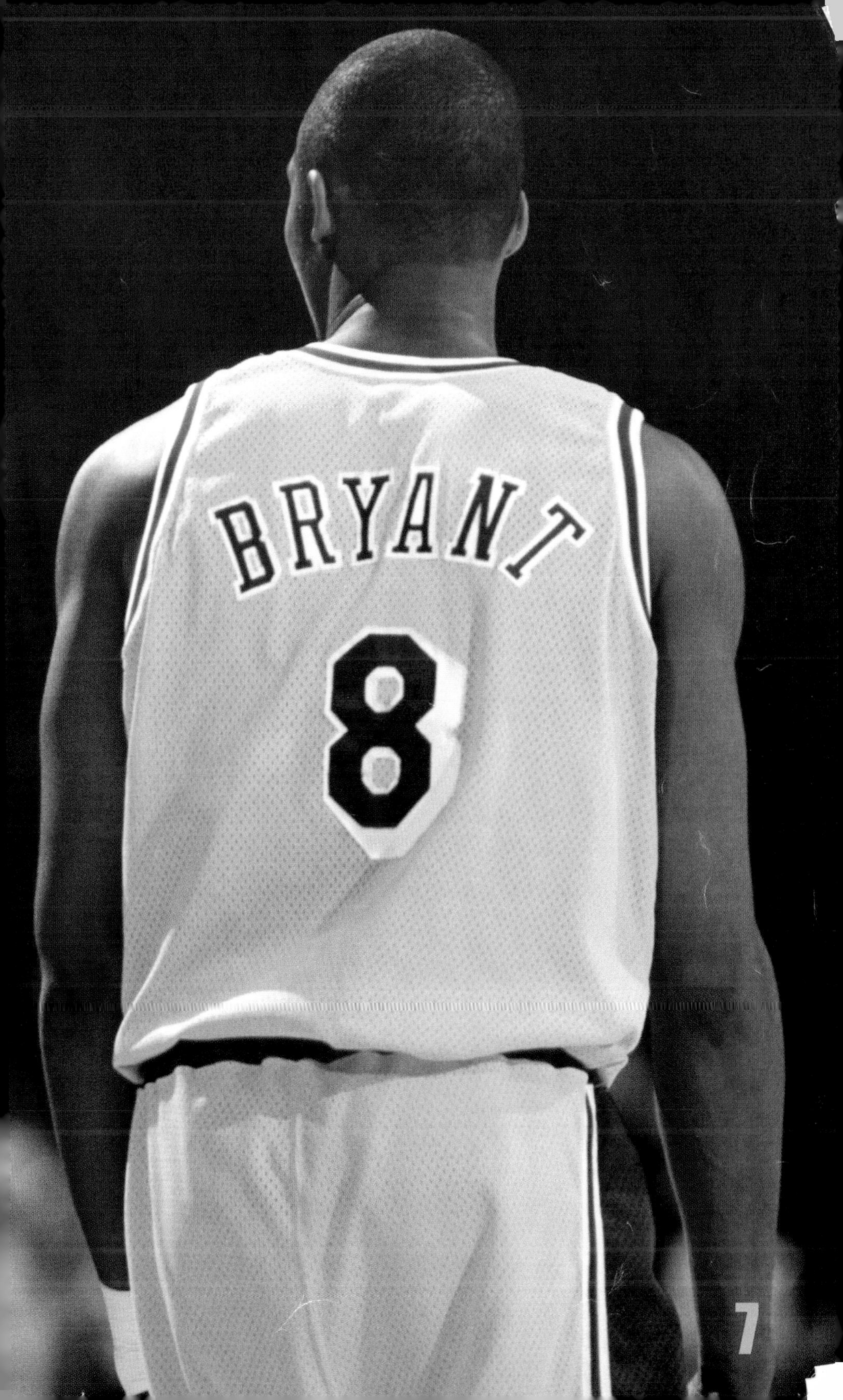
BRYANT
8

Kobe can jump way up in the air.

9

Kobe can reach up over players. He jumps high to get to the basket.

Kobe can dunk the ball. He can dunk the ball with one hand. People like to see him dunk the ball.

13

Sometimes Kobe uses two hands to dunk the ball.

In 1997, Kobe played in an All-Star game. It was a game for rookies. Kobe had a lot of fun.

Kobe and number 6, Eddie Jones, talked when they played in games.

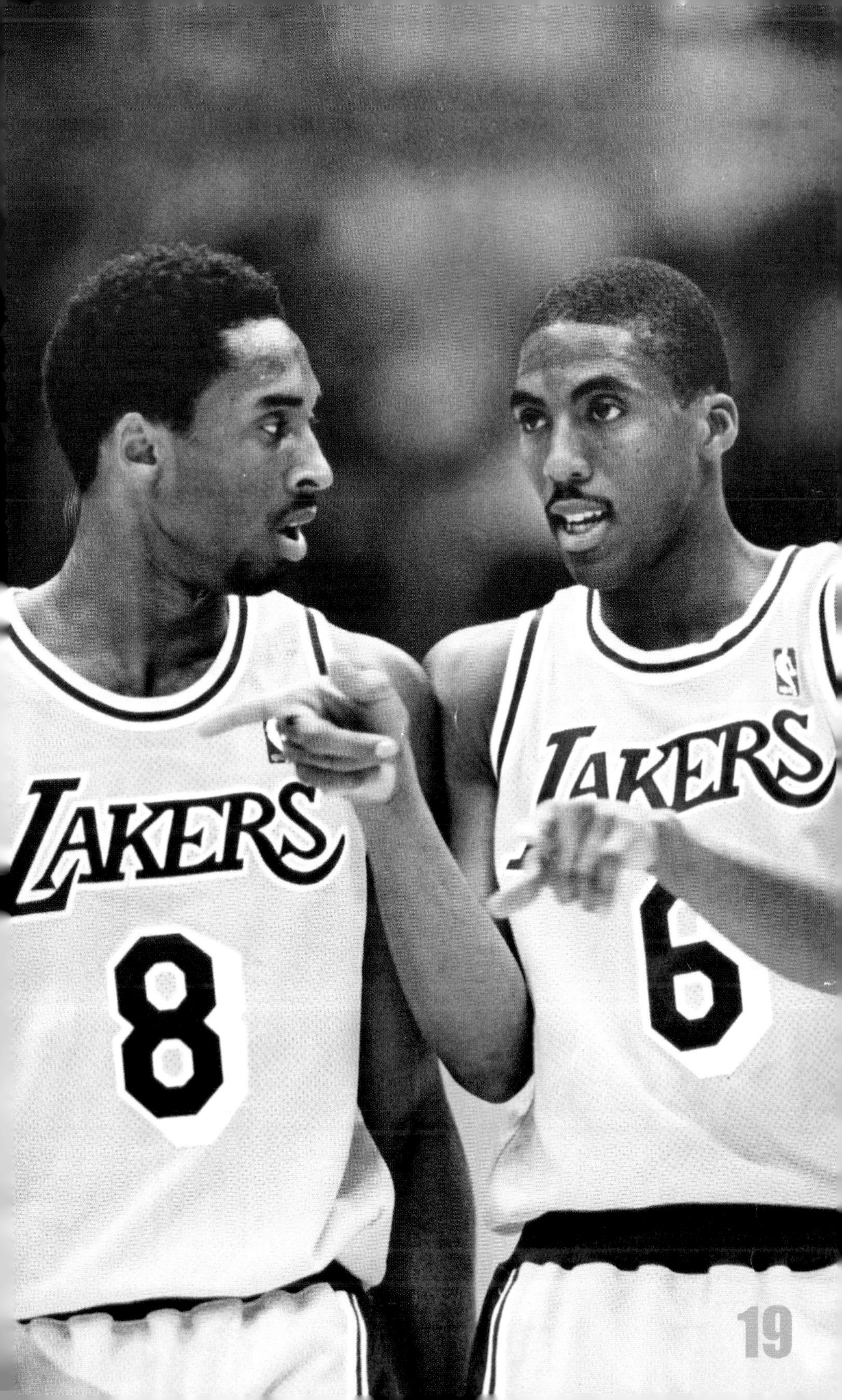
LAKERS
8
LAKERS
6

Shaquille O'Neal and
Kobe both play for
the Lakers.

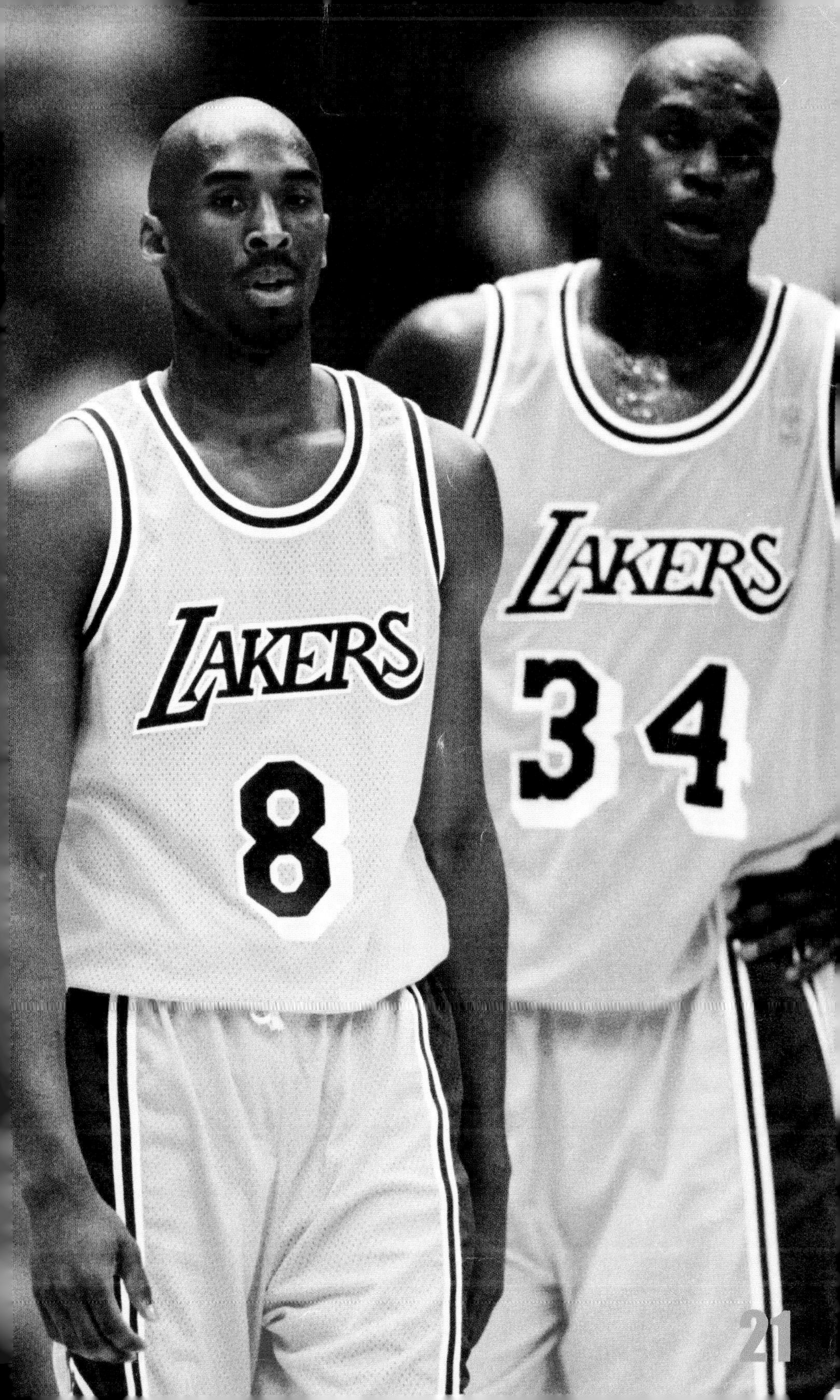
LAKERS
8
LAKERS
34

People like to meet Kobe.
They ask him to write his
name for them.

Here are more books to read about
Kobe Bryant and basketball:

Kobe Bryant
by Richard Brenner
Beach Tree Books (1999)

Basketball ABC: The NBA Alphabet
by Florence Cassen Mayers
Harry N. Abrams (1996)

To learn more about basketball, check
out this Web site:

http://www.nba.com/

Glossary

All-Star game (AWL STAR GAYM) A game for very good players.

dunk (DUNK) When a player reaches up and drops the ball right into the basket.

NBA (National Basketball Association) A group of players on different teams who get money to play basketball.

rookies (RUH-keez) New players.

Index

Word Count: 124

Note to Librarians, Teachers, and Parents

If reading is a challenge, Reading Power is a solution! Reading Power is perfect for readers who want high-interest subject matter at an accessible reading level. These fact-filled, photo-illustrated books are designed for readers who want straightforward vocabulary, engaging topics, and a manageable reading experience. With clear picture/text correspondence, leveled Reading Power books put the reader in charge. Now readers have the power to get the information they want and the skills they need in a user-friendly format.